MITCHELL SYMONS AND PENNY SYMONS

Illustrated by Jane Eccles

MACMILLAN CHILDREN'S BOOKS

www.panmacmillan.com

ISBN 978-0-330-51769-0

1 3 5 7 9 8 6 4 2

A CIP catalogue record for this book is available from the British Library.

Printed and bound in the UK by CPI Mackays, Chatham ME5 8TD

CONTENTS

neuf

INTRODUCTION

Hello and welcome to a very special book. This is a book for nine-year-olds that's actually *about* nine-year-olds.

You have something in common with every other boy and girl who's reading this book: you are nine years old. (If you're not, then you should stop reading right now!)

A lot of people – especially the sort of grown-ups who forget that they were once children themselves – think that being nine is just about going to school and playing at home. But sometimes nine-year-olds do extraordinary things, and you'll find out about them in this book.

As you read the stories and marvel at the trivia, remember that the people in this book were all nine when they did something memorable – just like you.

Make the most of this year: you'll never be nine again!

TECHNOLOGY AND INVENTION

When he was your age, Thomas Edison built a laboratory in his family's cellar in Ohio. He grew up to become a great inventor.

Edison was frightened of the dark, so it's fitting that he went on to invent the electric lamp!

In 2009, nine-year-old Lim Ding Wen from Singapore wrote a finger-painting program called Doodle Kids.

The program allows iPhone owners to draw images on the handset's touch screen using just their fingers.

The program was an immediate hit – being downloaded more than 4,000 times from Apple's iTunes store in the first two weeks it went on sale.

'I wrote the program for my younger sisters, who like to draw,' says Lim. 'But I am happy that people like it.'

TECHNOLOGY AND INVENTION

YOUR AGE IN DIFFERENT NUMERICAL SYSTEMS

Babylonian

Chinese

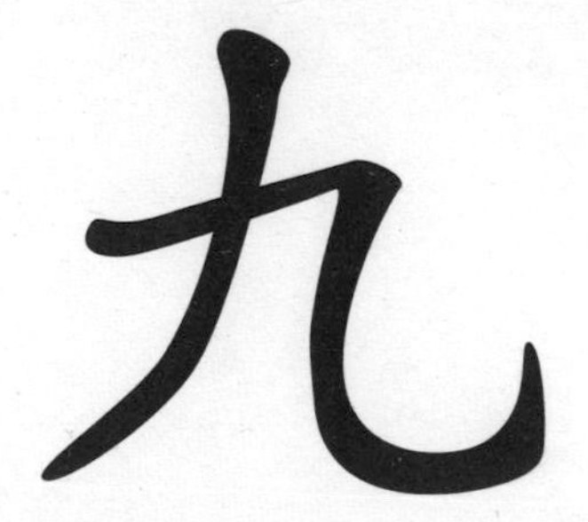

Counting rods

Cyrillic

Egyptian (hieratic)

Greek

Inuit

Mayan

Roman

MUSIC

When Beyoncé Knowles was nine, her father encouraged her and her friend LaTavia Roberson to start a band. That band eventually developed into Destiny's Child.

Lorin Maazel, one of the most famous classical-music conductors in the world, was conducting at the age of nine.

Alexandra Burke, who won the fifth series of *The X Factor* in 2008, was given a recording contract with Simon Cowell's record label. When she was nine years old, she sang on stage in Bahrain with her mother, Melissa Bell.

By the age of nine, Taylor Swift, the pop and country singer, was already determined to be a singer. Within a year she was performing locally and writing her own material.

When she was your age, Kylie Minogue was already a TV star in Australia.

At your age, Jimmy Osmond, the youngest member of the singing Osmond family, became the youngest person ever to top the UK singles chart – with 'Long Haired Lover From Liverpool'. It was the Christmas Number One in 1972 and the bestselling single of the year.

Christina Aguilera made her first TV appearance at the age of nine on a talent show called *Star Search*.

Legendary country singer Dolly Parton first appeared on the radio when she was nine. When she was ten she was a regular on the *Cas Walker Show*.

When she was nine years old, the singer and songwriter, Amy Macdonald, taught herself to play the guitar after picking up one of her father's many guitars. He had stopped playing them himself, but had been in a band when he was younger. Amy had no formal lessons, just a good ear for music, and she found a few chord patterns she liked the sound of on the Internet and taught herself to play them.

At first she would just play tunes she loved from the radio, but then she started to write and play her own songs.

The famous composer Sergei Prokofiev wrote an opera at the age of nine.

The great classical composer and pianist Franz Liszt played his first public concert at your age.

The pianist and composer Felix Mendelssohn gave his first public performance at the age of nine, when he reeled off a whole concerto *from memory*!

Vanessa-Mae is one of the world's top concert violinists. At the age of nine, she was not only performing but also composing her own solos – even while accompanying works by composers as great as Mozart! A year later, she participated in her first concerto performance, with the London Philharmonic Orchestra.

Michael William Balfe was a child prodigy who gave his first public concert in Dublin when he was nine years old.

He wrote his first composition when he was just seven years old and composed twenty-eight operas in his lifetime.

British violinist Nicola Benedetti became the youngest person in the UK to lead an orchestra at your age.

Two years later, Nicola performed at a memorial service for violin genius Sir Yehudi Menuhin in Westminster Abbey. She was nominated for two Classical Brit awards only a year after signing her very first record deal, which was worth a million pounds! In 2004, she won the BBC Young Musician of the Year award.

NINE YEARS IN AN ANIMAL'S LIFE

You are, of course, nine years old. You could easily live until you're one hundred. Other animals don't live as long. Take the camel. The longest a camel lives is fifty years or half a human life. So nine years in a camel's life means twice as much to them as it does to us. This means that a nine-year-old camel is really eighteen! Well, sort of!

Let's look at other creatures:

If you were an elephant, you'd be twelve years old.

If you were a macaw or a camel, you'd be eighteen years old.

If you were a donkey or a crocodile, you'd be nineteen years old.

If you were a horse, you'd be twenty years old.

If you were a lion or a deer, you'd be twenty-six years old.

If you were a bull, you'd be thirty-three years old.

If you were a pigeon, you'd be thirty-five years old.

If you were a wild pig, you'd be thirty-six years old.

If you were a tiger, cow or rattlesnake, you'd be forty-one years old.

If you were a cat, you'd be forty-six years old.

If you were a wolf or a blackbird, you'd be forty-nine years old.

If you were a small dog, you'd be fifty-three years old.

If you were a sheep or a goat, you'd be sixty years old.

If you were a large dog, you'd be eighty-four years old.

If you were a fox, you'd be sixty-five years old.

If you were a chicken, you'd be sixty-nine years old.

If you were a rabbit, you'd be one hundred years old.

If you were a queen bee, you'd be 180 years old or dead.

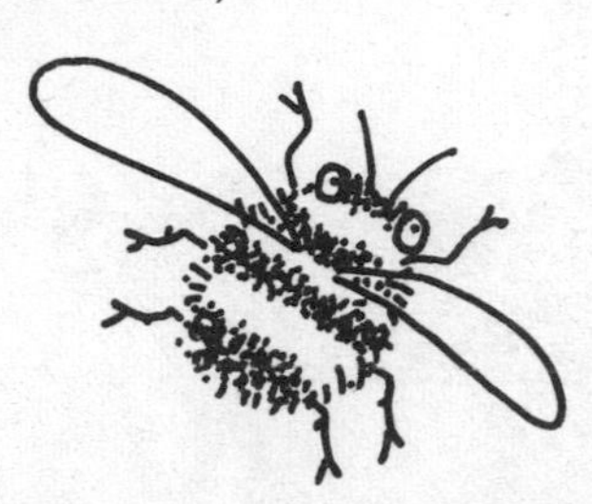

If you were a mouse, you'd be 300 years old and probably dead.

If you were a worker bee, you'd be 900 years old and definitely dead.

If you were an ant, you'd be 1,800 years old and most definitely dead.

If you were a mayfly – which lives for just one day – you'd be 328,725 years old and, yes, very much dead!

On the other hand, if you were a Galapagos turtle (which lives to 200 and beyond) you'd be just four and a half years old.

PRODIGIES

Antonin Michel amazed everyone in 1987 when he won the Junior World Scrabble Championship – at the age of nine (the upper age limit for the competition was fifteen).

Antonin Michel is French, so he plays Scrabble in his own language. But he can also play and compete at a high level in English. However good you are at languages, it must be difficult to play Scrabble in a foreign language!

He went on to win the World Championship in 2005 and again in 2007.

At your age, March Tian Boedihardjo, an Indonesian-Chinese boy living in Hong Kong, became the youngest child to pass maths A-level with a top A grade.

People don't normally take A-levels until the age of eighteen – in other words *twice* your age. Not surprisingly, March was offered a place to study the subject at Hong Kong's Baptist University.

Ruth Lawrence took A-level maths at the age of nine and got an A. She went on to get a first-class degree from Oxford University when she was thirteen.

$x = \frac{-(-2) \pm \sqrt{((-2)^2 - 4 \times 1 \times (-4))}}{2 \times 1}$
$x = \frac{2 \pm \sqrt{20}}{2}$
$x = \frac{-b \pm \sqrt{(b^2 - 4ac)}}{2a}$

Microsoft

At your age, Arfa Karim Randhawa of Faisalabad in Pakistan officially became the youngest Microsoft Certified Professional in the world. As a result, she was invited by the Microsoft boss, Bill Gates, to visit the Microsoft headquarters in America.

Arfa first got interested in technology when her dad bought her a computer. When she grows up, she would love to study at Harvard in America, work in a company like Microsoft and then go back to Pakistan to get involved in technological innovations in the field of satellite engineering.

ROYALTY

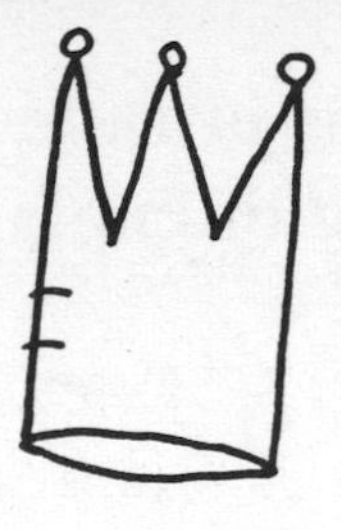

Many years ago in 1224, Princess Eleanor, the daughter of King John and Isabella of Angoulême, was married at the age of nine!

Henry III was just nine years old when he became King of England in 1216.

Edward VI became King of England at the age of nine in 1547. Edward was the only son of King Henry VIII, who had six wives over the course of his life. That's five more than most kings!

Lady Jane Grey was nine years old when she was sent to the royal court under the care of Queen Katherine Parr, the sixth wife of Henry VIII.

Lady Jane was later crowned Queen of England, but she reigned for only nine days! She was replaced by Queen Mary, the rightful heir to the throne.

Our queen's mother, Elizabeth, first met the man who was to become her husband when he was nine years old. It was at a children's party in posh Mayfair in 1905, and she was only four years old!

Queen Elizabeth II was nine years old when her grandfather King George V died. Normally this would have been quite unremarkable, but it turned out to be highly significant. Although she was born third in line for the throne, nobody dreamed she would one day become Queen of England. Her uncle, who became King Edward VIII, was obviously certain to marry and produce lots of male heirs and she would move down the line of succession. But then he decided to abdicate and this meant that her shy, stuttering father was crowned King George VI – and she, his firstborn child, was automatically heir to the throne.

King Louis XIII of France was crowned when he was just nine years old, though his mother ruled the country until he came of age at thirteen.

Margaret Beaufort was the mother of Henry VII, and the grandmother of Henry VIII. She was engaged to her husband at the age of nine.

SPORTS AND GAMES

Top golfer Justin Rose had his first hole-in-one at the age of nine, hitting a four-iron 122.5 metres into the cup at Tylney Park in Hampshire.

Wimbledon champion Pete Sampras began playing tennis at the age of seven. When he was nine, his father asked Pete Fischer, a physician and amateur player, to hit some shots with his son. Fischer was so impressed with the youngster's ability, he became his coach.

Sampras rarely won (major) junior tournaments, but did incredibly well as an adult.

Snooker champion Ronnie O'Sullivan achieved his first snooker milestone – a century break – at the age of nine. He was only fifteen when he became the youngest player to score 147, the maximum break possible.

The England rugby union player, Danny Cipriani, started playing rugby at school when he was nine years old. His mother Anne worked as a taxi driver to pay for his private-school fees. He also played junior football for Queens Park Rangers and was offered youth terms by Reading.

If that wasn't enough, he played schoolboy cricket for Berkshire and Oxfordshire, and was invited to join Surrey CCC (as a batsman).

England footballer Rio Ferdinand used to do ballet lessons as a child. However, when he was nine, he had to give it all up to prevent serious ligament damage which could have impacted upon his football career.

Wayne Rooney was signed by Everton's academy when he was nine. During one under-tens season, he scored ninety-nine goals.

Plenty of boys start playing competitive football at your age, but Gordon Strachan *managed* his first team at the age of nine. He persuaded his teacher to let him pick the class team! Gordon went on to play for Scotland, and eventually became a manager.

SPORTS AND GAMES

9

Ukrainian striker Andriy Shevchenko, a former Chelsea star, was just nine when the Chernobyl nuclear disaster forced him and his family to move from their home town.

They moved to escape the aftermath of radiation, but it was a blessing in disguise, because he was spotted by Dynamo Kiev!

French tennis player Richard Gasquet appeared on the cover of French *Tennis* magazine at the age of nine. He was the youngest Frenchman ever to be given a national ranking.

At the age of nine, Ashley Cole was spotted by Arsenal. He rose through the ranks to become not only a regular in the first team, but also an England star. He then moved to Chelsea.

When he was your age, Steven Gerrard was spotted by Liverpool FC scouts while he was playing for Whiston Juniors.

In 2010, at the age of nine, Zak Goodman from Uckfield, West Sussex, was awarded his black belt in SAMA karate. Zak reached this incredible goal after only four years of training.

'It is the best thing I have ever achieved and it feels really good,' he says. 'I like doing karate because it is fun.'

Florence Jackson from Bristol was nine years old when she became the first child ever to design a British coin for the Royal Mint.

Florence won a competition to design a coin to celebrate the 2012 Olympic Games being held in London. She beat a staggering 17,000 other entries to win the BBC Blue Peter competition.

At the age of nine, Judit Polgar competed in the New York Open Chess Tournament and took first place among unranked players.

Judit was born into a family of chess players in Budapest, Hungary. By the time Judit was five years old, she was already beating her father at chess.

Judit's parents educated their three daughters at home, with chess as their specialist subject. Each of them has several diplomas and speaks four to eight languages.

When she was your age, Maria Sharapova was picked out as a prospective tennis champion by the great player Martina Navratilova.

Maria left her home in Russia and began training at a tennis academy in America. She became the first child athlete to sign a million-dollar contract!

Sam Scholl was nine years old when he qualified for the Great Britain biathlon (running and cycling) team in 2007. He and two older swimmers from the Newbury Swimming Club took part in the World Championships in Monaco.

32 THINGS YOU SHOULD HAVE DONE BY THE AGE OF TEN

1. Make a mud pie
2. Roll down a grassy bank

3. Prepare a modelling-dough mixture
4. Collect frogspawn
5. Make perfume from flower petals

6. Grow cress on a windowsill
7. Make a papier-mâché mask
8. Build a sandcastle

9. Climb a tree
10. Make a den in the garden
11. Paint using hands and feet
12. Organize a teddy bears' picnic
13. Have a face-painting session

14. Bake some bread
15. Make snow angels
16. Create a clay sculpture
17. Take part in a scavenger hunt
18. Camp out in the garden
19. Bake a cake

20. Feed a farm animal

21. Pick some strawberries

22. Play Pooh Sticks

23. Find some worms

24. Recognize five bird species

25. Cycle through a muddy puddle
26. Create a mini assault course in the garden

27. Build a nest from grass and twigs

28. Find ten different leaves in the park

29. Grow vegetables

30. Plant a tree

31. Make breakfast in bed for your family

32. Make and fly a kite

How many have you done already?

AMAZING NINE-YEAR-OLDS

In 2006, nine-year-old Abby Goodall helped to save her mother's life.

When her mum suffered breathing problems, Abby stayed calm, dialled 999 and gave all the information needed to get help for her mum.

She received an award from the South East Ambulance Service. Her mum was very proud that her daughter had known exactly what to do in an emergency.

When he was nine, Ola Lauritzson from Sweden set up his own business – The Can. He collected used drinks cans and sold them to supermarkets.

Ola used the profits to buy shares in a Swedish sports company called Aritmos, and offered shares in his own company to his teachers, friends and neighbours.

At your age, he was hosting business meetings around his parents' kitchen table!

AMAZING NINE-YEAR-OLDS

In 2005, nine-year-old Johnny Wilson swam from Alcatraz Island to Aquatic Park in San Francisco. Alcatraz Island lies off the west coast of California, and once contained a tough prison that was notoriously difficult to escape from.

AMAZING NINE-YEAR-OLDS

Do you know what 'keepie-uppie' is? Even if the term is unfamiliar, you'll almost certainly know what it involves: keeping a football in the air – without letting it touch the ground - using just your feet, knees, chest and head. Graeme Lightbody is a master of this activity. In 2005, he beat his 2002 achievement of three hours fifteen minutes

with an incredible four hours thirty-three minutes at the Scottish Football Museum at Hampden Park, Glasgow. It was estimated that he achieved around 40,000 touches of the ball during that period.

The interesting thing about Graeme from our point of view is that he was nine when he first discovered his talent – managing an impressive 3,500 keepie-uppies.

How many can YOU do?

AMAZING NINE-YEAR-OLDS

9

In 2007, a nine-year-old golfing prodigy entered the *Guinness Book of Records* as the youngest girl ever to score a hole-in-one.

Rhiannon Linacre achieved the feat only three months after first picking up a club. She was playing at the Coxmoor Golf Club in Sutton-in-Ashfield, Nottinghamshire.

Rhiannon was younger than the previous record holder by seventy-six days.

In 2008, nine-year-old Ryan McLeish won the British 50cc standard quad-bike championship modified title. He had been doing the sport for less than two years!

In 1988, nine-year-old Emma Houlston made history when she landed her family's single-engine plane in St John's, Newfoundland, the furthest tip on the east coast of Canada.

Despite a shaky landing, the touchdown meant Emma was the youngest person to pilot a plane right across the whole of Canada. She was accompanied by her father, who was a licensed pilot.

It took Emma two weeks to make the journey. She flew from Victoria, British Columbia, 7,500 kilometres away on the furthest tip of the west coast.

9 AMAZING NINE-YEAR-OLDS

A nine-year-old boy called Vahe Hovhannisyan took over playing the organ every week at his local church in Connecticut in the USA when the organist announced that she wanted to give up.

Vahe was so small that he could hardly be seen behind the huge organ.

He played for two and a half hours every Sunday morning accompanying the choir and deacon for the service. He practised every weekday afternoon and learned how to play the music for weddings and funerals.

Joshua Schumacher was nine years old in 2002 when he climbed Mount Kilimanjaro, the highest mountain in Africa.

Joshua was probably the youngest person ever to climb the mountain, but it was officially an 'illegal climb'. The rules state that climbers must be ten years old before attempting to climb the mountain.

'WHAT DO YOU WANT TO BE WHEN YOU GROW UP?'

According to a survey of children of your age, the top ten ambitions are:

1. Sportsman/sportswoman

2. Pop star
3. Actor

4. Astronaut
5. Lawyer

6. Emergency services
7. Medicine

8. Chef
9. Teacher
10. Vet

ART AND LITERATURE

ART AND LITERATURE

Alec Greven was nine years old when he wrote *How to Talk to Girls*. The book was originally a handwritten school project, to show other boys in his school how to be confident when talking to girls. It was published as a book and soared up *The New York Times* bestseller charts.

Alec followed up his bestseller with *How to Talk to Moms* and *How to Talk to Dads*.

Bestselling author Jacqueline Wilson wrote her first novel when she was only nine years old.

Libby Rees is Britain's youngest published author, Her sixty-page self-help book, *Help, Hope and Happiness*, came out when she was nine. The book was based on her experiences when her parents separated. It raised thousands of pounds for the charity Save the Children, for which she is a youth ambassador.

Libby wrote a second book about her experience of moving up from primary to secondary school.

Peter Rabbit's creator, Beatrix Potter, was an unusual child. At the age of nine she was already a keen naturalist. Her fascination with plants and wildlife inspired her to become an artist. She was absolutely determined to draw the things she saw with great accuracy.

Beatrix's interest in animals led her to create her remarkable tales. She studied their behaviour very scientifically and used her skills as a painter to bring them to life.

ART AND LITERATURE

9

Ambia Khatun from Oldham, Lancashire, started writing her fantasy novel *Black Dragons* when she was nine years old. She completed the book in 2009, when she was fourteen.

Inspired by J. K. Rowling's Harry Potter series, Ambia's book is the first in a series of six. Ambia wanted to write a book with characters she could relate to as a young British Bangladeshi.

'When I started reading Harry Potter, I kept thinking how cool it would be to have a fantasy tale that had Asian characters in as well,' she says. 'The more I thought about it the more I wanted to write a book that me and my friends can relate to. There aren't many children's books that have Bangladeshi or Pakistani characters.'

Well, there's certainly one now!

Sir John Everett Millais was a nineteenth-century British painter and illustrator, and one of the founders of the Pre-Raphaelite Brotherhood. At the age of nine, he won a silver medal from the Royal Society of Arts for a drawing he did of the Battle of Bannockburn.

Millais was so talented that he won a place at the Royal Academy at the incredibly young age of eleven. While studying there, he met William Holman Hunt and Dante Gabriel Rossetti. Together, they founded the Pre-Raphaelite Brotherhood.

Can you imagine starting a school society that people would still be discussing more than a hundred years later?

AT YOUR AGE . . .

By the time you're nine, you will, on average, have . . .

blinked 59,458,500 times . . .

taken 75,555,000 breaths . . .

brushed your teeth 5,114 times . . .

watched 5,475 hours of television . . .

seen 225,000 TV adverts . . .

and farted 46,021 times.

You will have slept for 42,829 hours and 45 minutes . . .

grown to be 123 cm tall . . .

have an IQ of
100 . . .

and have
laughed
985,500
times.

FILM AND TV

Jack Lemmon was an Oscar-winning American actor who had the ability to be entirely convincing in both serious and funny films. His first lead role was in a school play at the age of nine. He forgot his lines and walked off to be prompted by a teacher. The audience laughed and so he did the same for every subsequent line. The audience loved it and a star was born.

At the age of nine, TV gardener Alan Titchmarsh was already a keen gardener. 'I could already see plenty of scope for improvement in our garden,' he says. 'I took cuttings of spider plants and geraniums and saved my weekly shilling pocket money to buy new seeds, such as alyssum, nasturtiums and Livingstone daisies. My limited resources meant that building up a bit of colour took a very long time indeed. I vividly remember being in Woolworth's once and seeing another boy of my age buy a propagator for half a crown. I wondered how on earth he had got the money.'

Cheryl Cole has gone from being a member of Girls Aloud to being a popular judge on *The X Factor*. However, when Cheryl was nine, it was her ambition to be a dancer. She joined the Royal Ballet summer school and went on to appear in a number of TV commercials.

At the age of nine, Austin Powers star Mike Myers appeared in his first TV commercial.

In 1993, nine-year-old Anna Paquin won the Best Supporting Actress Academy Award (Oscar) for her role in *The Piano*.

Elijah Wood is best known for starring in *The Lord of the Rings* films. But did you know that when he was your age he landed his first major role in the 1991 film *Avalon*?

Dame Elizabeth Taylor – twice the winner of the Best Actress Academy Award – made her film debut at the age of nine. Her family fled England in 1939 because of the beginning of the Second World War and Dame Elizabeth made her first film, *There's One Born Every Minute*, at the age of nine. Two years later, she starred in *National Velvet*, the film that made her a household name.

At the age of nine, Macaulay Culkin was cast as the lead character in *Home Alone*, the film which made him famous.

When actor Liam Neeson was nine, he took up boxing. He boxed for a team until he was seventeen. In one early match, his nose was broken and he had it set on the spot by his manager. That must have been painful!

Film star Orlando Bloom landed his first acting role when he nine. It was a brief scene in the TV hospital drama, *Casualty*.

Film star Christian Bale was nine when he gave his first big performance. He appeared in a play called *Nerds* with Rowan Atkinson.

Harry Potter star Daniel Radcliffe made his TV acting debut at the age of nine. He starred in a production of *David Copperfield.*

Sir Sean Connery was the first man to play James Bond in films. When he was your age, he had three jobs! He was working in a butcher's shop, doing a paper round and delivering milk to people's homes. He earned £2.50 a week.

Emma Watson was your age when she started the first of *eight* auditions that would lead her to landing the part of Hermione in the Harry Potter films. It was her first professional acting job.

When she was nine, *Britain's Got Talent* judge Amanda Holden was convinced that she was going to be a star. She was already practising Oscar acceptance speeches!

When *Strictly Come Dancing*'s Lilia Kopylova was nine, she was already an established ballet dancer, gymnast and figure-skater.

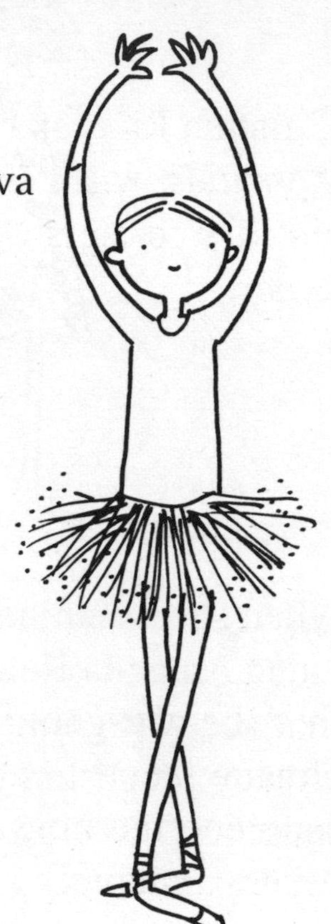

Christina Ricci starred in her first film, *Mermaids*, when she was nine years old. Her co-stars were Cher and Winona Ryder.

TV presenter Bruce Forsyth began dancing at the age of nine, after watching the films of the legendary American dancer Fred Astaire.

FUN FACTS

Most nine-year-olds get less pocket money these days than children did ten years ago.

A recent survey showed that most nine-year-olds are happy to help out in the house in return for pocket money.

At the age of nine, the average child knows 29,300 words. By the age of ten you will probably have discovered another 5,000 words – as long as you read lots of books!

At the age of nine, you need at least nine hours' sleep a night. However, ten hours' sleep is still the recommended amount for children of your age. Most nine-year-olds will fall asleep by nine o'clock and wake up at about seven o'clock in the morning.

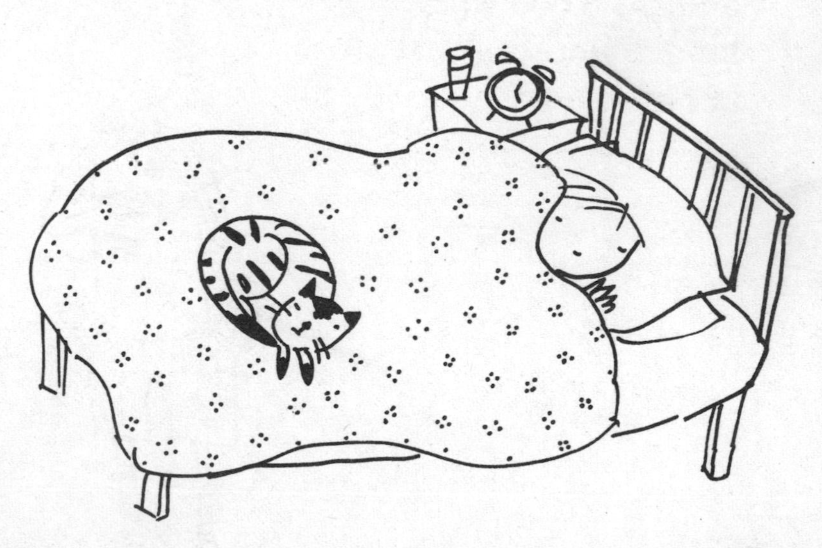

HISTORY

In 2010, a nine-year-old boy called Matthew Berger made one of the most important finds of all time: the fossilised collarbone of a child who lived almost two million years ago.

Matthew was out walking with his dad when he saw a fossil 'sticking out of a rock'. But it wasn't just *any* fossil! The bone that Matthew found belonged to someone very special indeed. Scientists now suspect that Matthew discovered a new species of human!

Researchers reported finding partial skeletons of the male child and an adult female who lived 1.78 million to 1.95 million years ago.

That's some find for a nine-year-old boy!

Lewis King, from Norfolk, was just nine years old when he enlisted as a soldier in the 1st Foot Guards in 1805.

The young lad ended up serving as a drummer in Lieutenant-Colonel Staples' Company in the 3rd Battalion at the Battle of Waterloo in 1815. He celebrated his nineteenth birthday in battle!

Lewis survived the battle and retired from army life at the grand old age of twenty-eight.

Annie Oakley was a famous American sharpshooter and exhibition shooter. She started using a gun when she was nine years old so that she could hunt wild birds for her family to eat.

Thanks to her shooting skills, she was able to sell the birds to local shops and restaurants. She was so successful that she paid off the entire mortgage on the family farm.

Annie Oakley gained lasting fame as a star performer in *Buffalo Bill's Wild West* show. Her life was made into a musical called *Annie Get Your Gun*.

HOW TO SAY 'NINE' IN DIFFERENT EUROPEAN LANGUAGES

Czech:
devět

Danish: ni

Dutch: negen

Estonian: üheksa

Finnish: yhdeksän

French: neuf

German: neun

Hungarian: kilenc

Icelandic: níu

Italian: nove

Latin: novem

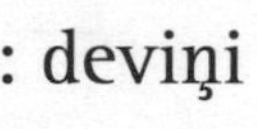

Latvian: deviņi

Lithuanian: devyni

Norwegian: ni

Polish: dziewięć

Portuguese: nove

Romanian: nouă

Slovak: deväť

Slovenian: devetih

Spanish: nueve

Swedish: nio

Turkish: dokuz

THE AGE CHILDREN SHOULD START SCHOOL IN DIFFERENT COUNTRIES

Age	Country
Four	Northern Ireland
Five	England, Malta, Netherlands, Scotland, Wales
Six	Austria, Belgium, Czech Republic, Denmark (seven until 2008), France, Germany, Iceland, Republic of Ireland, Italy, Liechtenstein, Norway, Portugal, Romania, Slovakia, Slovenia, Spain, Turkey
Seven	Bulgaria, Estonia, Finland, Lithuania, Poland (but kindergarten is compulsory from the age of six), Sweden

PHILIP ARDAGH'S BOOK OF HOWLERS BLUNDERS AND RANDOM MISTAKERY

Find out how the Pope got confused with a potato, about the footballer who ate the ref's notebook and why it's a terrible idea to get your name and date of birth tattooed on your neck in this splendid romp through the most impressive mistakes, blunders, misunderstandings, faux pas, howlers and universal truths that are not true at all!